A FOOTBALL CLUB IN PRESCOT

Glyn Williams

CONTENTS

Part One: Rise & Fall   1

Some Early Players & Matches   9

Part Two: From 'Athletic' To 'Cables'   16

More Notable Players   25

Conclusion   47

APPENDIX   49

BIBLIOGRAPHY   51

PART ONE: RISE & FALL (1884-1906)

It was in the Autumn of 1884 that a group of players from Prescot Cricket Club decided to maintain the sporting momentum by forming a football team and playing matches on a sloping field next door to the cricket ground on Warrington Road – the area now bounded by the railway line to the northwest, Warrington Road to the northeast, Ash Grove to the east and Hayes Avenue to the southwest. At the time the ground was owned by Lord Derby but is now given over to smart, redbrick, modern housing.

Plate 1: Aerial photograph of the Warrington Road ground (1929). The gate, cricket pitch, former football ground and spoil heap can be traced from top right to bottom left.

The footballers of 1884 were not alone in their enthusiasm for the new game. Clubs were proliferating across the country and there was talk of supplementing the FA Cup and other knockout competitions with organised leagues. In some of the industrial towns there was also talk of professionalism. Just four years later in 1888 twelve clubs from the northwest and midlands formed the Football League. It was followed in quick succession by a myriad of similar leagues across the country.

But for the time being the fledgling Prescot Football Club had to content itself with friendly matches against like-minded local teams. Its first match took place at home on Saturday, 29 November 1884 against St Thomas's Second Team, St Helens. For over a hundred years Prescot's matches were to be covered by the Prescot Reporter, and this opening game was no exception. I include only the opening section as quoted in Neville Walker's excellent history of the Prescot club *From Slacky Brow to Hope Street* (1990). Note the original writer's apparent unfamiliarity with football terms like 'corner', 'shot', 'heading' and 'offside'. His frequent reference to the ball as the 'leather' betrays the influence of cricket – hence the old expression 'leather on willow' meaning ball on bat.

The play was watched with much interest by a good sprinkling of spectators. The home captain [Wilkinson], having won the toss, chose to play uphill with the wind. The ball was set in motion by [Prescot's centre-half] Twist and in about five minutes from the start the leather was taken down the right wing and nicely passed towards the goal when the centre, Twist, put it between the uprights.

It was an own goal, by the way, and the goals themselves comprised two upright posts, a rope for a crossbar and no nets.

This caused the spectators to show their appreciation by cheering. Leadbetter [Prescot's centre-forward] kicked off, and again the ball was quickly in the home team's territory from which a 'corner' was obtained, but nothing was registered from this. Cookson [Prescot's goalkeeper] kicked out and for a few minutes the leather travelled quickly from one end of the field to the other but eventually Ellison [of St Thomas's] secured the ball and, after taking it some distance down the ground, made a 'shot' for goal but it hit one of the backs and rebounded into the field again, when Cousins [of St Thomas's] managed to evade the home custodian by 'heading' the leather past him, thus scoring a second goal. Again, Leadbetter set the sphere rolling, and after some desultory play, one of the home backs sent the ball well up the field and Prescot put the ball between the uprights. Before the leather had reached the goal, however, the whistles were blown for 'offside', so nothing resulted.

Prescot lost 3-0. The *Reporter* lists Prescot's team. Here it is presented in the old-fashioned 1-2-3-5 formation.

W. Cookson
Charles Wilkinson (captain), J.H. Sephton
Pearson Gill Twist, Joseph Case, N. Mercer
J.A. Baxter, J. Hunter, J. Leadbetter, J. Welsby and R. Woods

Of these, Charles Wilkinson later served as Prescot FC's secretary, treasurer and vice-president, P.G. Twist as president, Joseph Case 'had a lengthy off-the-field association with the club' (Walker), and Cookson was known for playing football in his cricket flannels.

Plate 2: An early Prescot FC team photograph. The striped shirts are probably blue and white.

Nicknamed the 'Watchmakers' and playing in blue-and-white stripes, the new club spent its first four seasons appearing in friendly matches and cup competitions. In September 1889 it played its first match in the Liverpool and District League, where in the ensuing years its opponents included, among others, Aigburth Vale, Aintree Church, Bootle Athletic, Bootle White Star Wanderers, Bromborough Pool, Earlestown, Kirkdale, Liverpool Stanley, Liverpool Reserves and local rivals Whiston. Its first trophy came in 1890 when it won the Liverpool Junior Cup after eliminating Bootle Victoria, Liverpool St Peter's, Newton, Garston Copperworks and Saltney Borderers – in a semi-final played at Aintree. It was a second replay and Prescot won 5-2. 'A huge crowd assembled at [Prescot] railway station to greet the 10 o'clock train carrying the returning team and their supporters,' Neville Walker recalls. 'As the locomotive steamed in, fog signals placed on the track by stationmaster Mr Prescott exploded "to add greatly to the enthusiasm". The victory was further celebrated at the nearby Eagle and Child Hotel with music provided by the Band of the 2nd Volunteer Battalion (South Lancashire Regiment). The final, played in May 1890 presumably, must have been a great disappointment by comparison, the team defeating its own reserve side 7-2 in a match played at the Prescot Bible Class Ground at Moss Meadow. The team competed in the FA Cup for the first time in 1891, losing 7-1 at home to Crewe Alexandra. The match attracted 3,000 spectators. 1891-92 saw them finish the season in third place in the Liverpool and District League after 'almost always hovering around the top four' (Walker). A year later Prescot FC got through the FA Cup 1st qualifying stage with a win at Rhosllanerchrugog (near Wrexham), after which defender Jack Woodward thought it best to escape to Ruabon Station in full kit rather than change and face a hoard of home fans accusing him of rough play. Prescot lost to Chester in the 2nd qualifier.

Prescot FC was elected to the Lancashire Alliance in 1895. This was a league comprising mostly teams in the county's southwest like Haydock, Earlestown, Skelmersdale United, Hindley, St Helens Recreation and Whiston. It lost only one home game during the ensuing season and finished fourth. The team had ended the previous season as losing finalists in the Liverpool Senior Shield. This year they clinched the trophy with wins against Whiston, Saltney Borderers, Bootle White Star Wanderers and, in the second of two finals played at the Liverpool Police Ground, Tranmere Rovers. Not surprisingly 1895-96 was also a success off the field, with the accounts showing a healthy profit of £5 15s 10d (about £5.80p – current value estimated at £615). After finishing runners-up in the Lancashire Alliance in 1897, Prescot FC was elected to the more prestigious Lancashire Combination, a league in which it would distinguished itself as the twentieth century unfolded. But not at this point. It finished the 1897-98 season second from bottom and returned to the Lancashire Alliance the following Autumn. Triumph came two years later in 1900 when Prescot was crowned Lancashire Alliance champions, notable wins, according to Neville Walker, including 11-1 against Peasley Cross and on the first day of the new century 6-1 against Seacombe Swifts. The success did not last for long. A year later, in 1901, the team ended up bottom of the Alliance and sent packing back to the Lancashire League.

Plate 3: The Hon. Arthur Stanley MP

Meanwhile plans were afoot to reorganise sport in Prescot. On 14 June 1902 a meeting was held in the Parish Rooms on Warrington Road to discuss the formation of a recreation club embracing cricket, football, cycling and athletics. Present were Lord Derby's son the Hon. Arthur Stanley MP (1869-1947), the Vicar of Prescot Harry Mitchell and members representing the sports involved. The meeting boasted plenty of committee members from Prescot FC. The issue involved a proposed extension of the Warrington Road ground, and the meeting ended with a resolution to form a special subcommittee, probably chaired by Rev. Mitchell, to work out specific plans for what most people would surely have regarded as a welcome development in the town's sporting life. Most but not all. Little is known about the reaction of Prescot's cyclists and athletes, but the football club was no doubt in favour of the plan. Not so Prescot Cricket Club, who clearly saw the development of the site as a threat. Their main concern centred on the fact that the ground was accessible only by a single gate located close to the railway bridge on Warrington Road (see Plate 1 above). This was fine for access to the cricket field, but the football pitch was located beyond the cricket field and close to what is now Hayes Avenue but at the time a colliery spoil heap known as 'Slacky Brow'. The spoil heap was no doubt linked to the colliery at Prescot Hall, at the bottom of what is now Hall Lane. For eighteen years (1884 to 1902) the cricket club had clearly been concerned about damage done to the northwest boundary, running parallel with the railway line, by football spectators making their way along the narrow path to the football pitch. (That crowd of 3,000 against Crewe Alexandra in 1891 would no doubt have unnerved members of the Cricket Club committee.) The cricketers also felt that the plan was too expensive. They turned it down.

Open hostilities broke out in August 1902 when the footballers were refused access to the ground for their first pre-season training session. The reason for the gateman's uncooperative behaviour was that Prescot FC owed the Cricket Club £7 5 shillings (£7.25p) access fee.

Just under £800 at current value, it was a considerable sum. Perhaps unreasonably, the cricketers also suggested that the Football Club should construct a twelve-feet-wide right-of-way path running along that northwest boundary. Neville Walker's account of the 1902 dispute makes no mention of how the footballers reacted to this idea. They did, however, own up to a debt of £1 5 shillings (£1.25p – about £125 now) 'which they fully intended to pay' but admitted no legal obligation to paying for access. Clearly they thought that Lord Derby's ground was tenanted jointly by them and the Cricket Club. The Cricket Club thought otherwise. Two days after their failure to train on the ground some footballers did manage to gain access. The gateman locked them in, forcing them to climb over the fence, and they were threatened with a summons for trespass by a Cricket Club committee member stepping 'out of the shadows' (Walker). The opening fixtures of both the first team and reserves were postponed. 'No … solution was found and the club did not fulfil season 1902-03 in the Lancashire League.' Walker ascribed it to Prescotian stubbornness:

Wills would have been too strong on both sides to permit any backing down…. the cricketers continued in sole occupation of the … ground for the time being, while the footballers … quietly sank into oblivion, albeit for a temporary period. The 18 year life of the original Prescot Football Club had, sadly, come to an end. It was to be three long and barren years before the resurrection of Prescot FC.

SOME EARLY PLAYERS & MATCHES

Neville Walker's account of Prescot FC's early years includes some bizarre matches – like the occasion in 1889-90 when all the balls burst and the game had to be abandoned; and a home match the following season when visitors Earlestown were trailing 2-0 at half-time, 'went into a collective sulk and refused to continue'. In one match at Bootle at this time the home club's tactics were spearheaded by 'an array of female beauty' – lovely young Bootle 'cheerleaders' aimed at turning the heads of the Prescot players while their team made advances of a different kind on the Prescot goal. It was an era when football was still in its infancy and anything could happen. This ran the full gamut from players entertaining the crowd with a little half-time dance routine, the light fantastic tripped by Jack Barlow and Joe Foster, versus Horwich, 1894-95, to the full-scale riot that broke out during a match at Whiston a year earlier. On this occasion Prescot's Jack Woodward put the ball in the Whiston net. Unfortunately, the Whiston goalkeeper was still holding it at the time. (Shades of Prescot's Bill Mercer playing for Huddersfield in the 1928 FA Cup Final when Blackburn's centre-forward Jack Roscamp bundled him over his line and the referee allowed the goal, and Harry Gregg's encounter with Nat Lofthouse in 1958.) The goal was disallowed but pretty soon all twenty-two players were embroiled in a punch-up. Then the 2,000 spectators joined in. Officials and police were unable to quell the riot and the match was abandoned. At a home match on Boxing Day 1892 the referee was attacked following an 11-2 defeat against Liverpool Reserves and the Warrington Road ground closed by the Liverpool FA for a short period in early 1893. (I'm beginning to understand Prescot Cricket Club's reservations about developing that sloping pitch next to Slacky Brow!) But the most bizarre match during this early period occurred in 1893-94 in the form of a friendly match between Prescot FC and the 'Prescot Darkies', a local minstrel troupe. Minstrel shows, in which white men coloured their faces with black boot polish and sang songs from the American Deep South, are unthinkable these days, but in the 19th and early 20th centuries they were extremely popular – among white audiences, at least. Writing decades before the invention of political correctness, the Prescot Reporter announced that 'the niggers' won 11-5. In the evening they put on a show at the Assembly Rooms (close to the old Royal Hotel on High Street).

Gat Lyon

Despite the valiant efforts of Neville Walker, we still know very little about Prescot's earliest players compared with the Roscoes, Whalleys, Jellys, Rainfords, Grisedales and Watkinsons of the 1930-60 period. All we know for sure about Gatley H. ('Gat') Lyon is that he was an accomplished right-back who captained Prescot FC in the late 1880s and early 1890s and at some point enjoyed a short spell with Liverpool Caledonians at their ground in Wavertree. He may have been part of the Caledonians team that won the Liverpool Senior Shield and played in the Lancashire League during the 1892-93 season. An unusual name like 'Gatley' is a God-send for genealogists. According to public records Gatley Henry Lyon was born sometime between April and June 1867 and according to the 1871 Census was the eldest child of William and Catherine Lyon of Irwell Lane, Runcorn, Cheshire. By the time of the 1891 Census Gat was a lodger living in St Helens Road, Eccleston and working as a Watch Barrel Maker. Three years later, in the summer of 1894, he married the twenty-year-old Emily Lyon with whom he fathered sons Cecil Henry (born 1897) and William Herbert (1898). Sadly, it's likely that Emily died giving birth to her second child. By the time of the 1901 Census Gat, the two boys and his sister Wilhelmina Margaretta (listed as 'Housekeeper Not Domestic') were living at 13 Lancaster Terrace (off Scotchbarn Lane), Prescot. Gat's profession is now described as 'Watchmaker Enamel Dial Maker'. The last available Census, published in 1911, reveals that Gat was working as an Electrical Fittings Inspector and living with his family a few doors along at 17 Lancaster Terrace. He died between April and June 1914 aged about 46. Wilhelmina Margaretta outlived her brother by 22 years, dying in Prescot aged 69 in 1936. The fate of Gat's two sons is unknown.

J. Hobbins

'Hobbins' is another unusual name welcomed by genealogists. One of Prescot's early goalkeepers was called 'J. Hobbins'. We don't know precisely when or for how long he played, but he did distinguish himself by scoring the 20th out of 23 goals against Liverpool Wanderers – Prescot's all-time highest score. I have traced what must have been this player's family back to the 1841 Census, when the widowed Mary Hobbins and her two small boys John and William were living with Mary's brother James Alcock in Houghton Street, Prescot. John was born c1833. If he was the 'J. Hobbins' who later played for Prescot he would have been in his early fifties when Prescot FC was formed. A more likely candidate might be found in three other members of the family. The first is James Hobbins, son of John's brother William, born c1861. Next comes another John Hobbins, James's brother and William's second son, born c1863. To make matters even more complicated a further John Hobbins appeared on the scene in 1868 – the son of John Hobbins I and his wife Mary. William's family remained in Prescot, living at different times at 4 Houghton Street (probably the house occupied by the Alcock family in 1841) and both 53 and 93 Kemble Street. Earlier in life they'd lived in Kemble Street when it was still called Hillock Street. Like Gat Lyon, the men in William's family were mostly connected with Prescot's watch-making industry: William and James as Watch Frame Makers and his brother John as 'Fusee' or 'Fuzee' (spindle) Makers. William's brother John was also a 'Fuzee' Maker. At the time of the 1881 Census he and his family lived at 42 Houghton Street, just nineteen doors or so away from William's brood, but spent most of their lives elsewhere. In earlier days they'd lived in Eccleston Street, Fall Lane (later Derby Street) and Plumb's Yard, Whiston, but by 1891 John and his family had moved to Oldham and the Lancashire cotton and iron industries.

Bill Robinson

The most successful Prescot player from this period was probably Bill Robinson. There is a photograph hanging in the Cables directors' lounge of players and officials gathered outside the Hope and Anchor Hotel during the 1913-14 season. The tall man on the rear right of the picture, wearing a flat cap and standing with his back to the drainpipe, has been identified by Neville Walker as Bill Robinson 'Scout from Hull City'. The Yorkshire club had been formed in June 1904 and in the ensuing years adopted the newly re-constituted Prescot Athletic as a sort of nursery club. As early as 1906 Prescot-born Walter Dagnall was playing for Hull City, and in the two years prior to World War One Sam and Jack Lyon (no relation to Gat as far as I know), Jimmy Middlehurst, Tommy Burns and goalkeeper Bill Mercer had followed suit. It is now clear that the connection between the two clubs was forged by Bill Robinson, who made 119 appearances for Hull (Football League Division 2) and scored six goals between 1905 and 1908 (Michael Joyce, Football League Players' Records 1888-1939). He also had spells at Manchester City (just one match, 1903), Bolton Wanderers (31 appearances, 1908-10) and Accrington Stanley (no details).

Plate 4: Prescot Athletic players and officials 1913-14 taken outside the Hope and Anchor Hotel. Ex-Prescot player and Hull City scout Bill Robinson is the tall man pictured immediately in front of the drain pipe and Jack Lyon and Tat Dagnall are seated on the front row.

William Samuel ('Bill') Robinson was born in Prescot sometime between July and September 1880. He was the seventh child of William Samuel Senior (c1845-99) and Esther nee Green (c1845-1917). They had been married in Eccleston on 16 February 1867 and at the time of the 1881 Census were living at 36 Eccleston Street, Prescot. William Senior is listed as a Joiner. By 1891 the family had moved to 37 Kemble Street and accumulated three more children, the ten of them ranging from three to 24 years old. Bill's father William died aged about 44 in 1899. In 1901 widower Esther Robinson and her family were living at 37 Kemble Street and Bill was listed as a Joiner's Apprentice. By this stage he was also a half-back with Prescot FC. By 1911 he'd completed his apprenticeship, risen to 'House Joiner Journeyman' and was living with his wife Margaret and six-year-old daughter Edna May at 41 Kemble Street. He'd married Margaret towards the end of 1903. Who was she? None other than Margaret née Dagnall, daughter of William and Mary Dagnall of 16

Duke Street and sister of Prescot players Bill, Joe and Arthur ('Tat') Dagnall. Bill Robinson died in Prescot in the early months of 1926 aged about 45.

After nearly four seasons in the cold, Prescot FC rose like a Phoenix from the ashes in time for the 1906-07 season. It also sported a new name (Prescot Athletic) and a brand new stadium accommodating not only the footballers but those cyclists and athletes thwarted by the dispute with Prescot Cricket Club in 1902. The Cricket Club continued to play at the Warrington Road ground until it was acquired for building purposes by British Insulated Cables in 1938, after which it moved to its present ground on Burrows Lane. In doing so it had exchanged what was probably an unattractive urban location for a rural idyll. The football club, on the other hand, had secured a ground close to the hustle and bustle of a busy industrial town centre. I suspect both clubs are still happy with this arrangement.

PART TWO: FROM 'ATHLETIC' TO CABLES' (1906-34)

The resurrection of the Prescot club in 1906 was due in no small measure to the Hon. Arthur Stanley who used his influence to acquire a plot of land at the junction of Hope Street and Eaton Street. The new stadium opened on 22 September 1906 with a cycling event followed a week later by Prescot Athletic's first fixture: a drawn game against Haydock Albion in the St Helens and District League. This inauspicious start did not last long, and by the end of the season Athletic had finished as runners-up and graduated to the Liverpool League. In those days players and officials changed in the Hope and Anchor Hotel until facilities were provided in an old barn closer to the pitch.

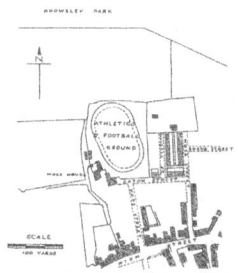

Plate 5: Prescot Athletic's new stadium, 1906
(from Neville Walker, Slacky Brow*)*

The opening few seasons in the Liverpool League saw Athletic holding their own, finishing third in 1907-08, seventh in 1908-09 and achieving 'a respectable placing' in 1909-10 (Walker). The key players in these early days were the young Jack Lyon, full-back Adam Middlehurst, goalkeeper Ned Whitehead, centre-half Ike Seddon and brothers Bill and Joe Dagnall. 1908-09 also witnessed the first ever fixture between Athletic and the Wire Works (British Insulated and Helsby Cables' works team). On this occasion Athletic lost 2-0 but they did go on to beat Halton Villa in the final of the Widnes Charity Cup. By the start of the 1909-10 season the Hon. Arthur Stanley MP had been installed as Club President and leading players included full-back George Jones, half-backs 'Wick' Hunter and Jimmy Lea, inside-forward Jimmy Scotson and Jack Lyon's elder brother Sam at centre-forward. As Neville Walker relates, vocal support from the Hon. Arthur Stanley MP and other members of the Knowsley Hall set helped to secure success in the match against Widnes Town in the Mersey Challenge Cup. Athletic lost in the next round – perhaps due in part to the absence of toffs from Knowsley Hall?

Not for the only time in the club's history, 1910-11 saw the team competing, on a fortnightly basis, in two leagues at the same time: the Liverpool League and the Liverpool County Combination. Athletic finished fourth in the Combination table, with a total of 30 points from 24 matches. Skelmersdale United were champions with 40 points and the Wire Works runners-up with 34. The season's first local Derby between Athletic and the Wire Works came on Saturday, 4 November 1911 and was heralded by an announcement published in both the Everton and Liverpool FC match programmes:

'Prescot Athletic ... meet their town rivals the Wire Works today, and there should be some rare sport at Prescot this afternoon, on this the first of the local "Derby" days' (Liverpool County Football Combination Handbook).

Refereed by W.E. Jones, the match ended in a 3-2 victory to Athletic thanks to a Jimmy Scotson hat-trick. The Athletic team comprised: Ned Whitehead; George Jones, Adam Middlehurst; Wick Hunter, Jack Eaton, Bill Prescott; Bill Dagnall, Jimmy Scotson, Sam Lyon, Peter Chorley, Arthur ('Tat') Dagnall.

1913-14 was a good season for Athletic. Goalkeeper Bill Mercer, Jack Lyon and Tat Dagnall returned after spells with St Helens Recreation and the team reached the semi-final of the George Mahon Cup. The first match against Southport Park Villa ended in a 2-2 draw, Prescot winning 3-0 in the replay. As Neville Walker explains, however, 'a further replay was ordered after an allegation that Prescot had fielded an illegible player was upheld.' Athletic lost the second replay 4-1. The team also fared well in the Liverpool Challenge Cup before losing 3-1 to Skelmersdale United in a semi-final played at Edge Lane, Liverpool. Their perfectly-respectable fourth position in the Liverpool County Combination was due in part to an amazing 40 goals scored by Walter Johnson between August and December 1913. His career was curtailed soon after when he suffered a bad shoulder injury. Walter retained his association with the club, becoming

Chairman in 1957. Back in 1913 his centre-forward position passed to Frank Mawdesley, who scored thirteen goals in five matches before fading from the picture.

   Though the Football League did not recommence until 1919-20, the Lancashire Combination was open for business from late 1918 and included the recently re-named 'Prescot FC' in its ranks. For the time being the Combination was split into two parallel divisions: one based in Liverpool and the other in Manchester. As expected, Prescot FC competed in the Liverpool section. The team was soon joined by Bill Mercer, Jack Lyon and Tat Dagnall, who had spent the 1914-15 season at Hull City and were now awaiting recall to Yorkshire for the imminent 1919-20 Football League season. The 1918-19 Lancashire Combination Liverpool Section was won by Tranmere Rovers, with Prescot runners-up five points behind. The club's first full season in the Lancashire Combination since 1897-98 ended with the Prescot FC's resignation – and for similar reasons to 1897-98. In both cases the club finished next to bottom of the Combination. Furthermore, travelling to some of the outer reaches of Lancashire proved expensive. A specific problem during the 1919-20 season occurred when a coach taking players and officials to Great Harwood suffered not only an engine breakdown but four burst tyres! The ensuing court case ordered the coach operator Joseph Cawley to pay the club £9 12s (about £432 today) in compensation. But the writing was on the wall, and a dignified return to the Liverpool Combination seemed the only option.

Prescot FC entered the FA Cup for the first time since the war in 1920-21, beating Harrowby in the first qualifying round but losing to Wrexham in the second. In the ensuing season the team finished eighth out of thirteen in the league, with 23 points from 24 matches. Burscough Rangers were champions with 39 points. By this time the running/cycling track had been removed and for the 1921-22 and 1922-23 seasons the Hope Street ground was shared with the Wire Works (playing in the West Cheshire League). Further ground improvements followed. The capacity was increased to a notional 15,000 (hard to imagine now), 'each spectator having a perfect view of the game' (Walker). Bob Monteith was the team's goalkeeper and was still playing 32 years later when he kept goal for Old Prescotians in the 1953 Boxing Day charity match. This fixture was originally instituted in 1922 when ex-Prescot players took on a Prescot Police XI. On this occasion the laurels went to the local constabulary, despite the efforts of Old Prescotians Jimmy Middlehurst, Peter Chorley and inside-forward Jimmy Scotson. The only accomplishment of the regular team in 1922-23 was reaching the semi-final of the George Mahon Cup. Presented to the Liverpool County Combination by Everton FC in memory of one of Goodison Park's founding fathers, the George Mahon Cup dated from 1909-10. Prescot won it in 1923-24, beating New Brighton 2-0 in a replayed final at Burscough, and again in 1926-27, when they defeated Marine 3-2 at Rake Lane, New Brighton. This occasion was marked by a celebratory tea back at the Busy Bee Café above Ames' grocery shop on Eccleston Street that concluded with laudatory speeches from an upper-floor window. Returning to 1923-24, this season also witnessed the first appearance at Hope Street of the Parish Rooms Band, who entertained spectators 'for almost 40 years, on and off' (Walker). When it was an 'off day' Prescot supporters and visitors sometimes enjoyed the musical stylings of the British Insulated and Helsby Cables Band 'conducted by Mr Boot'.

It should come as no surprise that in pre-TV days the fortunes of a local football team should have attracted the attention of local industry. As early as September 1926 John Evans, an official from the 'Wire Works' (by now plain 'British Insulated Cables Limited') travelled with club players and officials to an away match at Bootle Celtic and a month later Harry Lunt, another leading BIC official, revealed that he was 'an exceptionally enthusiastic Hope Street fan' (Walker). Prescot FC finished the season third in the Liverpool County Combination, taking 31 points from 23 games – four points behind champions Burscough Rangers and two behind runners-up New Brighton Reserves. Interest from BIC was also shown in January 1928 when ground improvements at the Eaton Street End were 'officially inaugurated' (Walker) by BIC directors. The opening ceremony was performed by Mr G. H. Nesbitt, the company's chief consultant engineer. According to Neville Walker, the company's directors were 'frequent visitors to the ground'. To put BIC's interests on a more official basis Captain Woods, the company superintendent, became Prescot FC's secretary. On the pitch, the team was player-managed by Jack Lyon and beat Liverpool 'A' 3-1 in the final of the Liverpool Challenge Cup. It was played at Goodison Park on 9 April (Easter Monday) 1928. The team retained it in 1929 and 1930.

Promotion and relegation issues are now clear-cut. In the English League system, teams finishing in the top one or two positions are automatically promoted while teams finishing just below engage in play-offs for the remaining promotion slot. Relegation issues, on the other hand, offer less chance of redemption, the bottom two or three teams axed mercilessly. Older readers will recall the days of Football League Division 4, when struggling teams were forced to undergo re-election at the end of the season, those not re-elected being replaced on an ad hoc basis by aspiring non-league teams.

    Elements of corruption and gerrymandering often infected the re-election process. The most flagrant abuse of the system concerned the promotion of Arsenal to Division 1 after World War One. The 1914-15 Division Two leaders and runners-up Derby County and Preston North End were promoted as normal but the third place went not to the teams in third, fourth or fifth place but to sixth-placed Arsenal – the result of a plot hatched by Football League President John McKenna and Arsenal Chairman Sir Henry Norris. In total contrast, Prescot FC's admission to the Lancashire Combination during the 1927-28 season was a triumph of endeavour and resourcefulness. In February 1928 Fleetwood went broke and resigned from the Lancashire Combination. Prescot applied to take over their remaining fixtures while at the same time seeing their season through in the Liverpool Combination. The ruling was that in order for Prescot to race both horses at the same time an entirely separate squad would be required for the remaining Lancashire Combination fixtures. A new set of players, including Jimmy Gray and James 'Paddy' Kane, was acquired 'in a few days' (Walker) and as in 1910-11 season the club fielded teams in two leagues simultaneously. The 'Lancashire XI' lost its first match against Southport Reserves but won at home against Wigan Borough Reserves, Atherton and Great Harwood, away at Bacup Borough and scored double victories against Burscough and Barnoldswick. The season ended with the combined Fleetwood-Prescot clubs 16th out of 20 with 30 points from 38 matches. 'Thus began … Prescot's "real" association with the Lancashire Combination which was to last for almost 50 years' (Walker). The 'Liverpool XI' finished third out of eleven with 28 points from 20 matches. The club's secure place in Lancashire ensured that never again would Prescot need to compete in the Liverpool Combination.

To celebrate their new status and endorse the considerable interest shown by BIC, the club changed its name to 'Prescot Cables' in time for the start of the 1928-29 season. It also adopted new team colours: black and amber stripes 'to commemorate a bit of local industrial history, as the first successful insulated cable drawn at Prescot was covered with black and amber paper' (match programme, A Brief History of Prescot Cables FC). The first phase of the new West Stand, a 1,000-seater structure built with money from BIC, was opened by the company's Managing Director G.H. Nesbitt before the first match of the season. By the end of the season the team had won the Liverpool Challenge Cup for the second of three successive years, beating Whiston 3-1 in a final played at Goodison

Park and witnessed by 6,000 spectators, and it finished fourth in the Combination, gaining 48 points from 38 matches. The club was on the crest of a wave, and together with Manchester North End, Mansfield Town and two other clubs applied for membership of Football League Division Three (North) in summer 1929. All five failed but the fact that Prescot Cables applied at all is evidence of its unbounded self-confidence. Two new wings of the main Hope Street Stand were opened by Football League Vice-President Charles E. Sutcliffe, dubbed by cartoonist George Greene as 'the prime minister of football', on 26 October 1929.

The team's performances in its first five seasons in the Lancashire Combination proved that its initial acceptance in 1928 was more than justified. Thanks no doubt to the leadership of former Liverpool stars Don McKinlay and Jack Bamber, the safe hands of goalkeeper Horace Whalley and the prolific goal-scoring prowess of Jack Roscoe, the team finished fourth in 1929, sixth in 1930 and runners-up in 1931, 1932 and 1933.

Plate 6: Cartoonist George Green's take on the opening of the new stand at Hope Street on 26 October 1929

MORE NOTABLE PLAYERS

Walter Dagnall's short career at Hull City started in 1906, when he played eight games and scored two goals for the Yorkshire team after spells with Prescot Athletic and St Helens Recreation. It is highly likely that Walter was a member of the same family as Bill, Joe and Arthur ('Tat') Dagnall though, as yet, I have found no link in birth, marriage, death and census records. Michael Joyce states that he was born in Prescot in 1883 and went on to play for Skelmersdale United and Rossendale. But there the trail ends. There was a Walter Dagnall born in Prescot in 1883 but with no apparent link to Bill, Joe and Tat. Sam Lyon, on the other hand, was playing for Hull City before October 1913 and his brother Jack by the same date. By Saturday, 29 August 1914 – 25 days after the declaration of war – Jimmy Middlehurst, Tommy Burns and goalkeeper Bill Mercer were also Hull City players. Neville Walker speculates 'it is unlikely that any of [these Prescot players] actually turned out for the Yorkshire "Tigers" before the war, since a total shut-down of the game "for the duration" was soon called.' For once Walker is mistaken. These men may not have played for Hull before the war but some or all of them might well have played for their new club during the war. Soon after the declaration of war on 4 August 1914 the gentlemen-amateurs of cricket and rugby union followed the call to arms and abandoned all hope of continuing 'for the duration.' The cricket contingency was so keen to fight for King and Country that they abandoned the 1914 season with only three matches remaining. The professionals of football and rugby league, on the other hand, with livelihoods at stake, decided to carry on. The 1914-15 season went the full distance in both sports. Everton won Division One, Derby County Division Two, Sheffield United the FA Cup (played well away from the conflict at Old Trafford), Celtic the Scottish League Division One, Eccles Borough the Lancashire Combination and Huddersfield just about everything up for grabs in Rugby League. Hull City ended the 1914-15 season in seventh place in Football League Division Two, with 43 points from 38 games. The Liverpool Combination also saw the 1914-15 season through to its conclusion though without Prescot Athletic. The league went ahead with just ten teams, Skelmersdale United finishing top and Burscough Rangers winning the Hall Walker Cup. The George Mahon Cup was abandoned after the first round.

The Lyons and the Dagnalls

The Lyon and Dagnall brothers made a deep impression on the pre-war Prescot team. When Athletic beat their local rivals the Wire Works 3-2 on Saturday, 4 November 1911 the team's line-up included not only hat-trick man Jimmy Scotson but

Sam Lyon at centre-forward and Bill and Tat Dagnall on the right and left wings respectively. Sam Lyon was the elder brother of John ('Jack') Lyon and was born on 20 November 1890. The brothers' parents were William Lyon, listed as a coal miner in the 1891, 1901 and 1911 census returns, and Elizabeth née Jaundrill (both born c1866) of Sewell Street, Prescot. His brother Jack was born on 3 November 1893. By the time of the 1901 census the family was living at 5 St Helens Road, Prescot and by 1911 at 16 Moss Street. The 1911 Census reveals that Sam, now aged 21, was working as a 'nurseryman labourer'. According to his recruitment c1909 to Territorial Force 5th Battalion South Lancashire Regiment, he was employed by James Whittaker & Son. Jack on the other hand is listed as a 'coal miner haulage below ground' in the 1911 Census. Michael Joyce reveals that Sam played six games and scored one goal for Hull City between 1912 and 1913 before playing eight games and scoring three goals for Barnsley in 1914. A Samuel Lyon married Nora Davies in Prescot between April and June 1916 but we cannot be sure that it was footballer Sam. There is little evidence of him after World War One.

His brother Jack, on the other hand, not only survived the war but went on to play for Hull City (37 league games and six goals between 1913 and 1919) and Leeds City (33 games and three goals in 1920) between spells at the Prescot club. He may even have been the Jack Lyon who turned out for Liverpool 'A' against Sutton Commercial in October 1921, scoring Liverpool's goal in a 2-1 defeat (information from Jonny Stokkeland of the Liverpool FC official archive website). Jack may have played for Prescot Athletic as early as his mid-teens (Walker suggests it could have been during the 1907-08 season when he would have been 14 or 15). His career also included spells at New Brighton (28 games and 5 goals in 1923), Derby County and Mold Town. By Easter Monday 1928 he was back at Prescot, player-managing and captaining the team that won the Liverpool Challenge Cup 3-1 against his old team Liverpool 'A'. A photograph of the victorious Prescot team shows him seated next to the trophy.

Jack retired at the end of the 1928-29 season after a twenty-year career playing at inside- and centre-forward across northern England and Wales. His position as captain passed to ex-Liverpool star Don McKinlay and, in turn, to McKinlay's Anfield team-mate Jack Bamber. Jack Lyon died in his eighties in 1975.

Plate 7: Jack Lyon (front row centre)

Bill, Joe and Tat Dagnall were the first, third and sixth children of William Dagnall and his wife Mary Chesworth. The couple were married at St John's Church, Liverpool on 4 August 1875. By the time of the 1901 Census Mary was a widow living with her seven children at 16 Duke Street, Prescot. Her first child Bill was born c1879, her third child Joe 1884 and her sixth child Tat 1889. Bill and Joe are listed as 'watchmaker finishers' while Tat was still at school. By the time of the 1911 Census, Bill, by then aged about 32, had married Rose McDonnell (St Silas's Church, Liverpool, 1908) and together with their young daughters Margaret and Mary were living at nearby 22 Duke Street, Prescot. Meanwhile at 9 Duke Street Joe is listed as the head of the family and Tat as a 22-year-old 'assisting in lead covering of cables'. Bill died sometime between July and September 1943, Rose following him 21 years later in 1964. Little is known about the middle brother Joe except that he was born c1884 and died in Prescot aged 81 in early 1965. A Joseph Dagnall married Elizabeth Allen in Prescot sometime between October and December 1945. Footballer Joe would have been about 42 years old and it is by no means certain that he was the bridegroom.

Of the three Dagnall brothers Tat seems to have made the most impact on the football pitch. He was born in 1889 and may well have been the Arthur Dagnall that married Esther Leadbetter in the spring or early summer of 1923 and died in Prescot aged 65 sometime between July and September 1954. His football career has been chronicled by Jonny Stokkeland. He played for Prescot Wesley Guild (FA amateur registration 4 October 1909), St Helens Recreation (professional registration 10 June 1912), Prescot Athletic (transfer registration 8 July 1913), had a trial with Hull City (probably 1913-14) and played in two Liverpool FC wartime friendly matches in the strictly unofficial 1916-17 season. As Jonny states, 'he played outside-left for Prescot against LFC Reserves on 5 October 1918' and signed for Liverpool in May 1919, his transfer from Prescot completed in April 1920. He played in 23 Central League matches and one friendly for Liverpool Reserves in 1919-20 and scored two goals. After a transfer to Whiston on 16 October 1920 he returned to Prescot two years later and retired from the game in 1926. Neville Walker characterises him as 'a brilliant little outside-left. Few men have given longer service to Prescot senior football'.

Bill Mercer

Of the many names listed in Neville Walker's coverage of this era, goalkeeper Bill Mercer was probably the most successful player in terms of a football career away from Prescot. He was born at 3 Cyprus Street, Prescot, on 27 May 1888 and baptised at St Mary's Parish Church the following 11 July. His parents were William Henry Mercer, a railway shunter, and his wife Martha. He had at least one brother: Peter Mercer, who served as landlord of the Hare and Hounds pub on Warrington Road (now Tommy Hall's) in the 1930s. His early years at Prescot are shrouded in uncertainty. According to Walker, Mercer, Jack Lyon and Tat Dagnall were 'welcomed back [to Prescot] after spells with St Helens Recs' but it is unclear when they'd played for Prescot previously. Mercer was certainly in the squad for the 1913-14 season, and his imposing figure can be seen, on the back row dressed in a white jersey, in the Hope and Anchor photograph mentioned above (see back cover). On 29 August 1914 he was transferred to Hull City. After 193 appearances for the Yorkshire team, Mercer was signed by Huddersfield Town's legendary manager Herbert Chapman in 1924 and was a key member of their 1924-25 championship side. It was a season in which the team never conceded more than two goals in any match. Mercer made 79 appearances for Huddersfield, including the 1928 FA Cup Final, his team losing at Wembley 3-1 against Blackburn Rovers. It took place just five weeks before his 40th birthday and was his last appearance for the club. By the start of the ensuing season, he'd moved to Blackpool, where he stayed for just one season and made nineteen appearances. He died in 1956 aged about 68.

Plate 8: Bill Mercer on an extremely soggy pitch

Don McKinlay

Defender Don McKinlay was born in Glasgow on 25 July 1891 and learned his craft with local teams Newton Swifts (the name by which Rangers' reserve team was known) and Newton Villa before legendary Liverpool manager Tom Watson signed him, aged nineteen, on 27 January 1910. He made his debut the following April in a remarkable match against Nottingham Forest that Liverpool won 7-3. The highlight of McKinlay's sixty appearances for Liverpool before World War One must have been the FA Cup Final against Burnley at Crystal Palace on 25

April 1914. In front of a 72,778 crowd, Burnley won 1-0 thanks to a goal after 57 minutes from ex-Everton player Bert Freeman. It was the first FA Cup final played in the presence of a reigning monarch (King George V) and the last one played at Crystal Palace.

When the Football League resumed after the war McKinlay became a key figure in Liverpool's defence. He was appointed captain in 1921 and during the ensuing seasons led the team to two successive championships (1921-22 and 1922-23). For a natural leader he wasn't tall, standing at just 5 feet 9 inches, but weighed 11 stone 9 pounds and was certainly no push-over. It was during his first championship season that he won two caps for Scotland: against Wales at the Racecourse Ground, Wrexham on 4 February 1922 and a month later on 4 March against Northern Ireland at Celtic Park, Glasgow. McKinlay was primarily a tough, hard-tackling defender but, like his spiritual descendant at Cables Harry Grisedale, he was capable of moving up front and scoring goals, especially from free-kicks. 'McKinlay ran up, and with a fierce drive such as he alone is capable of sent the ball flying into the left-hand portion of the goal,' the *Liverpool Echo* reported on a match against Oldham on Boxing Day 1922. 'In the matter of shooting nothing is more remarkable than the way Donald McKinlay continues to score goals'. His most remarkable goal came at West Ham on 16 January 1926 when he hoofed the ball in from ten yards inside the Liverpool half: a distance of sixty to seventy yards! Though McKinlay never maintained his pre-war rate of 24 goals in 136 matches, his official career total of 34 in 433 matches is well above average for a defender scoring only four times from the penalty spot. His career at Anfield ended abruptly following an injury sustained in a 4-3 victory at Villa Park on Saturday, 7 January 1928.

Plate 9: Don McKinlay as a young Liverpool player

After nineteen years of faithful service McKinlay's contract at Anfield ran out in July 1929. He was quickly snapped up by Cables, playing for them during the 1929-30 and 1930-31 seasons. He featured mostly at left-back and proved, I suspect, an inspirational captain. He held strong views about captaincy:

In my day I had full control on the field and if there was any decision on changing of positions, I took it. ... I told my players: 'If I have to say anything to you, [don't] answer me back and don't start sulking'.

Looking at photographs of McKinlay in his prime it is easy to compare him with some of the great captains of later Liverpool eras, notably Liddell, Yeats, Smith, Hughes, Hansen and Gerrard. Little is known about his private life. There are a number of 'Donald McKinlays' to be found in local family records, ranging from the Donald N. McKinlay who married a Miss Gordon in Liverpool in late 1929 (he would have been 38) to the

Donald J. McKinlay who married Kathleen Newman in early 1958? What we do know is that when our man wasn't working as a publican in Liverpool after retiring from the game in 1931 he enjoyed an occasional round of golf and playing the drums. He died on 16 September 1959 aged 68.

Plate 10: St Helens-born Jack Bamber as a young man

Jack Bamber

One of Liverpool's players during the glory days of the early 1920s was the tall, dark and imposing Jack Bamber, who followed a successful career at Anfield with spells at Leicester City and Tranmere Rovers and two seasons at Prescot Cables (1930-32), succeeding his ex-Liverpool team-mate Don McKinlay as captain in 1931. Jack was born in Peasley Cross, St Helens on 11 April 1895, the son of a glassworks grinder named Robert Bamber and his wife Mary. At the time of the 1901 Census Robert and Mary were living at 97 Napier Street, St Helens and had three sons and two daughters: Joshua (born c1888), Elizabeth (c1891), Robert (c1893), John (who was six at the time of the Census) and Victoria (c1898). After several seasons with St Helens Recreation, where he may well have played alongside Bill Mercer, Jack Lyon and Tat Dagnall, he turned out for Alexandra Victoria, Heywood (probably during its days in the West Lancashire League) and St Helens Town (see Michael Joyce, Football League Players' Records 1888-1939), Bamber was signed by Liverpool in 1915 but had to wait for the resumption of league and cup football in 1919 to make his debut. He made 72 appearances for Liverpool and scored two goals. It was during this time that he made his one and only appearance for England, playing at left-half against Wales at Ninian Park on 14 March 1921. He was transferred to Leicester City in 1924, staying there until 1927 (seven goals in 113 appearances) before moving to Tranmere (one goal in 86 matches). He captained Cables during two of their early-30s runners-up seasons (1930-31 and 1931-32). Jack died in St Helens aged 76 on 26 May 1971.

Horace Whalley

The match between Prescot Cables and Lancaster Town in September 1930 is long forgotten except for the performance of one particular player: Cables' 21-year-old goalkeeper Horace Whalley. The football correspondent of the *Prescot and District Reporter* praised his 'parrying, fisting and kicking away all kinds of shots, including a penalty.' 'Bobbing up and down like a cork,' a Lancaster supporter present at the match commented, he was *'nobbut a little 'un, but he's a good 'un!'* In the same way that Frank Garton was custodian supreme of the Cables' goal during the 1950s, Whalley dominated the goalmouth for most of the 1930s, and only a world war curtailed his claim to be Cables' greatest ever keeper.

Plate 11: The 1931-32 team. Jack Bamber is seated next to Jack Roscoe (front row centre pair) and in front of Horace Whalley.

Horace Walter Whalley was born in Prescot on 29 March 1909, the son of John and Eleanor Whalley, who were both born in 1886. All we know about his parents is that in 1924 they took over management of the Bath Springs Hotel on Kemble Street. At about the same time their teenage son appeared in goal for Rainhill Recreation. Horace represented the 'Recs' for two seasons during which they remained unbeaten and conceded just eleven goals. At the age of sixteen (c1925) he joined Whiston AFC and a year later was playing for Everton Reserves. Not retained at Goodison, Whalley signed for the Cheshire County League club Harrowby aged seventeen or eighteen (c1926/7).

He joined his hometown team Prescot Cables in time for 1929-30 – the same season that witnessed Don McKinlay's arrival at Hope Street. Whalley was very much the unpaid apprentice. His first two seasons at Hope Street were quietly successful, the team finishing fifth in the Lancashire Combination at the end of 1929-30 and runners-up in 1930-31.

Whalley's sterling service was rewarded in March 1931 when he was selected for a Liverpool County FA XI. He played for the LCFA XI several times during the ensuing years. Following a 'trifling difference' with Cables' management (unpublished notes from Walker's *Slacky Brow*), Whalley returned to Harrowby, his place between the Cables sticks passing to Jimmy Trill. In 1933 Trill was ruled out of action by a severe dose of influenza and Whalley stepped in as temporary keeper. Appearances for Cables during this brief sojourn included a 5-1 away defeat at Nelson that marked future England wartime international Frank Soo's last appearance before seeking fame at Stoke City. Whalley's next port of call was Prescot BI (the Wire Works' successors), where he made a name for himself as a penalty taker, scoring from the spot twelve times.

For the three seasons between 1933 and 1936, Cables sought what Neville Walker called 'a new sphere of influence' in the Cheshire County League, an event heralded by the return of Horace Whalley, this time not as an unpaid apprentice but a paid master. Records from these three seasons in the Cheshire League are sparse but it is clear that Horace made a vital contribution to the team. 'Whalley was in particularly brilliant form ... [and] amazed the crowd' (Walker). The Prescot and District Reporter remarked that his 'absolute finesse compelled [the home crowd] to applaud his efforts ... when he came out of the dressing room after the change round. Whalley received a great ovation. On Saturday's display, he deserves a quick passage to any First Division club'. But a call from the top flight was never received.

Saturday, 23 September 1935 was a monumental day for Whalley. In the morning he married Margaret Birchall at Prescot Parish Church and in the afternoon played in the 10-0 thrashing of his old team Harrowby in an FA Cup Preliminary Round match at Hope Street. Local cartoonist George Green was on hand to chronicle the event, ingeniously fusing the idea of wedding and football match to comic effect. The ten goals are shown as ten grinning balls each wearing top hats, and Cables centre forward Jack Roscoe is hailed as the Best Man for scoring six of Cables' goals.

Plate 12: Whalley's Wedding Day

As that Lancaster Town supporter implied a few years earlier, Horace Whalley was not a big man. He had neither the height of six-feet-four-inches Harry Nickson, who kept goal for Cables in the late-1940s, nor the robust frame of Nickson's successor Frank Garton. But his compact physique and sharp features were heaven-sent for George Green and that other local cartoonist Bert Wright. Occasionally, of course, his relatively slight figure suffered at the hands of big, aggressive centre forwards. Men like ex-Bolton and England star Joe Smith (later manager of Blackpool during the Matthews Era), who Horace faced in a match against Manchester Central during his first spell at Cables. Smith charged Whalley so fiercely that *'the goalkeeper finished unconscious in the back of the net and it took a couple of trainers and an ambulance man to bring him round!'* (Walker).

As his parents' long spell in charge at the Bath Springs came to a close, an eye injury kept their son out of the Cables line-up between Spring 1936 and Easter 1937. He was sorely missed, Cables conceding over a hundred goals during the period. By October 1937 he was 'back to his brilliant best' (Walker) and in the ensuing November the *Liverpool Echo* reported that Cables were lucky to have such an experienced player as Whalley. On 26 February 1938 he assumed the role of Cables' penalty-taker, converting a spot-kick in a thrilling 3-2 defeat against South Liverpool at Hope Street. Cartoonist Bert Wright captured the occasion in one of his amusing pictorial match reports.

Plate 13: Whalley the penalty-taker

After a well-deserved benefit match in May 1938 (Cables versus South Liverpool again), when Horace was 29 years old, he 'was playing as well as ever' (Walker) during the ensuing 1938-39 season. He did not play in any of the three Cables matches that preceded Neville Chamberlain's declaration of war on Sunday, 3 September 1939, though, keen to play as ever, he did turn out for Prescot BI against Earlestown Bohemians at the end of the month. Nothing is known of Horace's war service. He was aged 30-36 during the conflict.

Like so many other Cables' players, among them Bill Rainford, Fred Finney and Sandy Lyon, Horace was more than an outstanding footballer. He was also a talented all-round athlete, 'engaged in running, jumping, tennis, cricket and billiards in his time' (Walker). It must have been painfully frustrating when, in 1946, he suffered an accident at work that resulted in the amputation of his left foot. In an undated clipping from the *Prescot and District Reporter* (kept at the Prescot Museum), Bert Taylor reports on Whalley's welcome appearance in the vice-presidents' stand at Hope Street.

Horace, well known in Prescot for his sporting qualities, was only recently discharged from Whiston County Hospital ... Despite his handicap, he has, happily, managed to retain his cheerful disposition, and in answer to my inquiry regarding his welfare, said: 'I will feel better when I get something stuck on the end [of my leg]'. For many seasons, Horace was a popular member of Prescot Cables' playing staff and was regarded as one of the most brilliant goalkeepers in the Lancashire Combination. His valuable services to the club will long be remembered. It is pleasing to note that, as a vice-president, he still takes a deep interest in the club, and supporters will join me in expressions of good luck for his future.

Virtually nothing is known about his later life. He died close to his 68th birthday sometime between January and March 1977. Rather surprisingly, his death was registered in Greenwich, London.

Jack Roscoe

'One of the greatest goal scoring centre forwards who ever played for Lancaster Town, for South Liverpool and for Prescot Cables' (Neville Walker).

When the FA changed the offside rule in time for the 1925-26 season, thus reducing the number of defenders between the lead attacker and goal from three to two, an avalanche of goals ensued. The total number of goals scored in the Football League increased by just under 36%. In the English First Division the increase was 43%. That's a rise of just over one goal per game. The new era witnessed the emergence of high-scoring superstar centre-forwards like Dixie Dean of Everton, who broke the First Division record in 1927-28 (the third season played under the new rule) by scoring 60 league goals. His overall total for Everton, between 1925 and 1938, was 349 goals in 399 matches or a goal in 86% of matches played. Not that his scoring rate went unchallenged. His contemporary Hughie Gallacher of Newcastle, Chelsea, Derby and Notts County scored 275 goals in 388 matches or a goal in 72% of matches played. Other First Division target men of the period include Gordon Hodgson of Liverpool, who scored 233 goals in 358 matches (a goal in 63% of matches played) and Birmingham's Joe Bradbury (249 in 414 matches – 60%). An almost identical pattern emerged in the Lancashire Combination, where goals increased by almost 42% - also just over one goal per game. And there was a centre-forward similar to Dixie Dean: a man who in the ten seasons between 1929 and 1939 scored in the region of 512 goals, including124 for Lancaster Town and over 190 each for Prescot Cables and South Liverpool. His name was Jack Roscoe.

Jack Roscoe was born in Prescot on 22 October 1909 and registered in the 1911 Census as a one-year-old child residing at 3 Saggersons Court, on the east side of Moss Street. The Victorian courts of Moss Street are long gone and now replaced by small housing estates. They include Aron Court, Rio Court and Seddons Court, the last named after the bakery and grocer's shop formally on St Helens Road. Saggersons Court occupied the area now devoted to Seddon's Court.

According to the 1911 Census, 3 Saggersons Court was a six-room dwelling. Jack's parents were William Roscoe (1867-1944), a mechanic specialising in making watch tools, and Elizabeth née Whittle (c1870-1929). Jack had six brothers: James (born c1892), an assistant glass bottle blower; Thomas (born c1894) and Samuel (born c1896), who both worked as 'carrier to the bottle blower'; William Baden Redvers (born c1901) and Joseph (born c1903), who were still at school; and Nathaniel (born c1908), a three-year-old still living at home. (William Baden Redvers Roscoe's extravagant name was no doubt inspired by those two military heroes of the Second Boer War Lord Robert Baden Powell and Sir Redvers Henry Buller.) Jack also had four sisters: Sarah Jane, who was born about 1893 but died aged 18 shortly before the census took place (her name is scratched from the record), Lilian Anne Jane, (born 1899), Elizabeth (born c1906) and Margaret (born after the census in 1917). The Prescot Roll of Honour website reveals that his elder brother Thomas served in the South Lancashire Regiment in World War One. By the time of Thomas's military attestation in December 1915 the family had moved to Beesley Cottages, St Helens Road, a house they still occupied at the time of Jack's wedding to Lucy Welsby in late 1934.

Jack was educated at Prescot Council School on Warrington Road and, judging from a photograph shown to me by his daughter Pat Sumner, served as a Boy Scout. His main football experiences as a boy were with Prescot Rangers. A team photograph dated 1924-25 shows him in what was to become his usual No.9 position. It was a season in which Jack scored 84 goals, a club record broken only by Bill Watkinson just before World War Two. (In 1957 Bill beat Jack's Cables record of 64 goals.) A brief press clipping shows that at the age of nineteen Jack, like Horace Whalley, had signed amateur forms with Everton, the official 1927-28 reserve team photograph showing him in the No.7 position. According to Michael Joyce, however, Jack never played for the first team. But Joyce does record Jack's time at New Brighton: five goals in sixteen games in the 1929-30 season.

Plate 14: George Green on Roscoe as Horace Whalley's 'best man'

He arrived at Prescot Cables, whose ground was located a literal stone's throw from home, in time for the 1930-31 season. He was reunited with his old friend Horace Whalley, the two youngsters enjoying the privilege of playing alongside veteran defenders Don McKinlay and Jack Bamber (see above). While Whalley was stopping goals at one end of the pitch Roscoe was finding the target regularly and often at the other, scoring 59 first-team goals in 1930-31. (The record of 64 goals in a season at Cables mentioned above is a little misleading since five of them were in reserve matches.) Jack's goals included a hat-trick in a Lancashire Junior Cup replay at Horwich RMI: a foretaste of many more hat-tricks to come. The first half of the following season was spent at Rotherham United. Despite finishing the 1930-31 season 14th in the Third Division North, Rotherham had struggled to be re-elected and obviously keen to recruit a high-scoring centre-forward. The acquisition of Roscoe did not work out, Jack scoring just three goals in five games. Back at Cables in late 1931 or early 1932, Jack scored an astonishing 50 goals 'in little more than half a season' (Walker). For the third year running Cables finished the 1932-33 season as Lancashire Combination runners-up: second to Darwen in 1931 and 1932 and to Chorley in 1933. Roscoe finished the 1932-33 season with another 50-goal haul, making 159 goals in all. Players and management must have asked themselves the question, 'Where do we go from here?' For the ensuing 1933-34 season the club decided to try its fortunes in the Cheshire County League, Roscoe with Lancaster Town.

*Plate 15: Jack Roscoe during his early days at Cables
(by kind permission of his daughter Pat Sumner)*

Jack went on to score 124 goals for Lancaster Town between 1933 and 1935, setting a new Lancashire Combination record of 67 goals in 1934-35. His return to Cables in the summer of 1935 was surely linked to the birth of Jack and Lucy's first child Joan in May 1935 – at about the same time that his team was celebrating their Lancashire Combination championship. Holding down his job at BIC in Prescot (where he worked as a crane driver) with matches in Lancaster and beyond must have put a lot of strain on the emerging Roscoe family. After scoring 27 goals for Cables between August 1935 and January 1936 he was transferred to up-and-coming South Liverpool, where in the ensuing three-and-a-half seasons he scored a total of 190 goals and his team won a staggering eight trophies: three Lancashire Junior Cups (1937, 1938 and 1939), three Lancashire Combination championships (also 1937, 1938 and 1939), one Lancashire Combination Cup (1939) and, best of all, the Welsh Cup in 1939. And forget about goals coming in hat-tricks, fours and fives. On at least five occasions Jack scored six goals in a single match: three times for Lancaster and once each for Cables and South Liverpool. By the end of the 1938-39 season South Liverpool had achieved an unprecedented quadruplet, following on from the previous season's personal achievement of Jack beating his own Lancashire Combination goal record by scoring 75 goals. The birth of his second daughter Eileen in early 1938 and third child Pat in May 1939, making three children under the age of five, prompted Jack to return to Cables. He played in just one match, scoring two goals at Bacup Borough on Tuesday, 29 August. War was declared five days later and soon after that the nation's football programme closed down for the duration. Jack was 36 when demobbed from the Royal Navy in 1945. As far as I can see his post-war football was limited to the annual Old Prescotians versus Prescot Police charity matches every Boxing Day and a little scouting for South Liverpool. Jack Roscoe died in October 1996, a few days either side of his 87th birthday.

CONCLUSION

When the Prescot club reached its centenary in 1984 the occasion was marked by a players' re-union dinner organised by club president (and as a journalist working on the Prescot Reporter its chronicler) Bert Taylor, an event graced by many of the club's greatest names from the 1930s, 40s and 50s. These included Jack Roscoe, Bert Jelly, Sandy Lyon, Harry Grisedale, Frank Garton and Bill Watkinson. It is not known if a similar event was organised to mark the club's 50th anniversary in 1934. Probably not. This book has attempted to put flesh on the bones of Prescot's first half century, tracing it from its origins as an adjunct to the local cricket team to a successful and respected member of one of England's most distinguished non-league setups. Compared with the 1920s, when the team won five trophies in six years (see Appendix below), 1934 wasn't a particularly successful year for the team. Its best player Jack Roscoe was away scoring goals galore for Lancaster Town, and the team's switch to the Cheshire County League was already proving a mistake. (It was an era dominated by the newly-emerging Wigan Athletic, which won the Cheshire League in 1934, 1935 and 1936 while Cables finished the same seasons fifth, 17th and 18th respectively.) Thankfully, Cables were welcomed back to the Lancashire Combination in 1936 with open arms. Overall, the combined Prescot FC-Cables-Town team completed 45 seasons in the Lancashire Combination. It played 1,476 games and scored 2,823 goals (nearly two goals per game). More importantly, it accumulated 1,398 points in the league (just under a point per game), making it the tenth most successful team in the league's 91-year-old history. After World War Two it enjoyed fifteen years of unprecedented success, winning the Lancashire Combination Cup in 1948, the Lancashire Combination Championship in 1957, the Liverpool Senior Non-League Cup in 1952, 1953, 1959 and 1961, and in 1957 and 1959 it reached the first-round proper of the FA Cup. At the time of writing the team is playing in the Evo-Stik League Division One North – the eighth of 22 levels in the English league system. The team ended the 2016-17 season a few points clear of relegation. But the last match of the season witnessed a great achievement: a 1-0 home victory against Southport in the final of the Liverpool Senior Cup. Prescot's football club is still alive and kicking!

APPENDIX: PRESCOT'S TROPHIES
1884-1934

1890	Liverpool Junior Cup
1895	Liverpool Senior Shield
1899-1900	Lancashire Alliance
1909	Widnes Charity Cup
1924	George Mahon Cup
1927	George Mahon Cup
1927	Liverpool Challenge Cup
1928	Liverpool Challenge Cup
1929	Liverpool Challenge Cup

SELECT BIBLIOGRAPHY

Joyce, Michael: *Football League Players' Records 1888 to 1939* (Soccer Data Publication, 2012).

Laschke, Ian: *Rothman's Book of Football League Records 1888 to 1978-79* (Macdonald and Jane's, 1980).

Liverpool County Football Combination handbook (undated).

Walker, Neville: *From Slacky Brow to Hope Street* (Knowsley Central Library, 1990).

Williams, Glyn: *'The Dixie Dean of Non-League Football: Jack Roscoe (1909-96)'*, in The Non-League Magazine, Issue 8.

Williams, Glyn: *'Lancashire Hot Pot: a history of one of England's most celebrated leagues'*, in The Non-League Magazine, Issue 12.

www.rsssf.com/tablese/englancacombhist.html (for comprehensive Lancashire Combination league tables)

Printed in Great Britain
by Amazon